North American
Historical Atlases

FIRST

FRONTIER

George Caleb Bingham painted this vision of Daniel Boone leading settlers through the Cumberland Gap.

North American Historical Atlases

FIRST FRONTIER

Rebecca Stefoff

BENCHMARK BOOKS

MARSHALL CAVENDISH
NEW YORK

Benchmark Books
Marshall Cavendish Corporation
99 White Plains Road
Tarrytown, New York 10591

• • •

Library of Congress Cataloging-in-Publication Data
Stefoff, Rebecca, date.
First Frontier/Rebecca Stefoff
p. cm—(North American Historical Atlases)
Includes bibliographical references (p.) and index.
Summary: Chronicles the exploration and settlement of lands west of the
Appalachian Mountains during the late 1700s and early 1800s.
ISBN 0-7614-1059-7 (lib.bdg.)
1. Frontier and pioneer life—United States—Juvenile literature.   2. United States—Territorial expansion—Juvenile
literature.   [1. Frontier and pioneer life.   2. United States—Territorial expansion.]   I. Title.
E179.5 .S815   2001   99-047936   973.5—dc21

• • •

Printed in Hong Kong
1 3 5 7 8 6 4 2

• • •

Book Designer: Judith Turziano
Photo Researcher: Matthew Dudley

• • •

Contents

Chapter One

BEYOND THE MOUNTAINS

During the 1600s the colonies of British North America were huddled along the Atlantic seacoast, where the ocean was their link to the Old World of England and Europe. But in the 1700s, as the colonies grew larger and more crowded, American colonists began to turn their eyes westward. The unknown land beyond the Appalachian Mountains, they believed, was endless, rich with **game** and good soil, and theirs for the taking.

The Proclamation of 1763

As the westward push began, the French and British were fighting over the Ohio River Valley west of the Appalachians. French traders from Canada had established good relations with the Native American people, or Indians, of the Ohio Valley. France's goal was to gain control of the center of North America, from the Great Lakes south along the Mississippi River to the Gulf of Mexico. This would let France block the British colonists' attempts to move westward and keep them penned in their narrow coastal strip between the Atlantic and the Appalachians.

War between France and Great Britain broke out in 1756. In North America this conflict was called the French and Indian War because most Indians sided with the French against the British. The worst fighting took place on the western **frontiers** of Virginia, Pennsylvania, and New York, where bands of Native Americans—urged on by their French allies—attacked and burned homesteads and killed settlers.

In the end, the British defeated the French, who were forced to give up Canada. But some Native Americans, fearing an onrush of British settlers, continued to fight. Their leader, an Ottawa chief named Pontiac, declared, "I mean to destroy the English and leave not one upon our lands." The British defeated Pontiac's followers, too, and by the summer of 1763 Great Britain claimed the Ohio country. Hoping to prevent more fighting between Native Americans and settlers, the British government ordered that settlers could go no farther west than the top of the Appalachian Mountains. This declaration, called the Proclamation of 1763, was supposed to be a barrier to westward movement until the government could figure out how best to administer its new western territory.

The Mountain Wall

If the Proclamation of 1763 was an official barrier to westward **migration**, the Appalachian Mountains were a physical barrier—and an impressive one. Stretching for 1,200 miles (1,931 kilometers) from eastern Canada to central Alabama, the Appalachians are not a single mountain range. They are a group of ranges: the White Mountains of New Hampshire; the Green Mountains of Vermont; the Catskills of New York; the Alleghenies of west-

Settlers who crossed the Appalachian Mountains had to carry all of the tools and supplies they would need to carve a homestead from the heavily forested wilderness.

ern New York, Pennsylvania, and West Virginia; and, farther south, the Blue Ridge, Great Smoky, Cumberland, Black, and Unaka Mountains.

The Appalachians are not very tall, as mountains go. Their highest point, Mt. Mitchell in North Carolina, is 6,684 feet (2,037 meters) — less than half the height of many peaks in the Rocky Mountains of the West. But to colonists on the coastal strip the Appalachians were high enough to be forbidding. They were also extremely rugged, with range after range of steep hills and brush-choked valleys as far as the eye could see, all densely wooded. Hunters and explorers who ventured into the mountains claimed that their two most valuable possessions were their axes, for clearing paths, and

THE SPECULATORS

The Proclamation of 1763 angered land-hungry American colonists itching to stake their claims on the western side of the mountains. None were angrier than the land **speculators**, as real-estate investors of the time were called. They operated by obtaining title to huge tracts from the colonial governments that claimed to own the land and then selling small parcels of it to individual farmers for much more than they had paid for it. Land speculation was so profitable that speculators sometimes paid to build roads to carry settlers to their properties.

Some companies of speculators had received grants of land west of the Appalachians from the colonial governments, and the Proclamation of 1763 made them afraid that the British crown would not honor these claims. A few speculators found legal loopholes that let them buy and sell land despite the Proclamation, while others obtained their land grants directly from the crown. Among the famous colonial Americans who made fortunes in land speculation were George Washington, Patrick Henry, and Benjamin Franklin.

their rifles, for hunting game and shooting hostile Indians.

"Men of the Western Waters"

A lot of ordinary men and women paid no attention to either the Proclamation of 1763 or the land speculators—they simply crossed the Appalachians on their own and carved homesteads out of the wilderness. During the 1760s, most of them crossed the Allegheny Mountains in Pennsylvania and settled near Fort Pitt, which is now Pittsburgh. They used the Forbes Road, a wagon track between Philadelphia and Fort Pitt that the British army had created to supply the fort during the French and Indian War. After the war, the Forbes Road guided settlers west to the beginning of the Ohio country.

By the mid-1700s there were about 35,000 white settlers living in what was officially Indian territory west of the Appalachians. They called themselves "men of the western waters" because most lived near rivers or streams that were both water sources and highways for their boats, rafts, and canoes. But these tough, independent settlers were not the only people living in the region. The original inhabitants of the area were not yet willing to give it up.

Indian Resistance and the Fight for Kentucky

Hunters, settlers, and speculators soon moved into the region called Kentucky, west of

Rivers and streams provided more than water. They were highways for frontier travelers—
but they also presented dangers such as ice, rapids, and swift currents.

Pennsylvania and south of the Ohio River. The Shawnee Indians who hunted there grew alarmed, realizing that once Kentucky was populated it would no longer support their traditional way of life. The settlers, however, saw the land as empty. In their eyes, if it didn't have European-style farms and villages, it wasn't being used.

Tension between the Shawnee and the settlers broke into open fighting in 1774. Lord

A note on John Filson's 1784 map of Kentucky thanks "Dan'l Boon" [sic] and others who shared geographic information with the mapmaker. The land north of the Ohio River is labeled "Indian Territory," but Filson could not resist adding a note near "Old Shawnee Town" to point out the quality of the "excellent land."

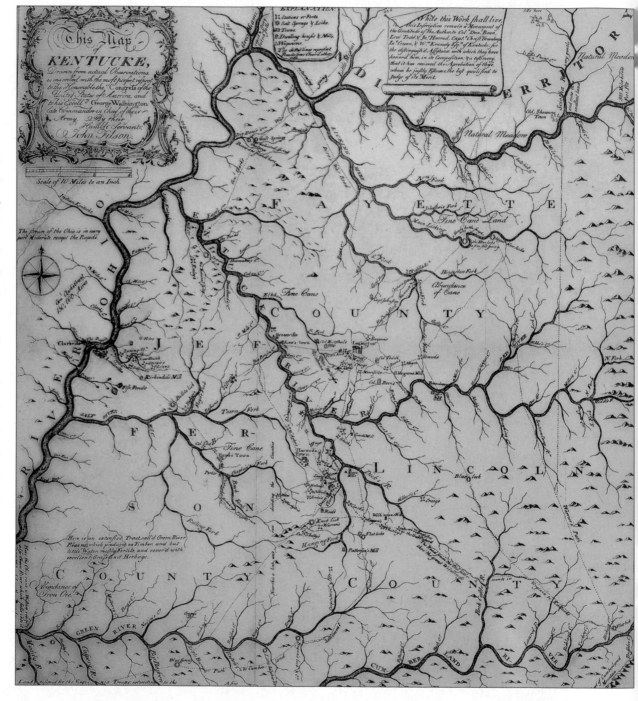

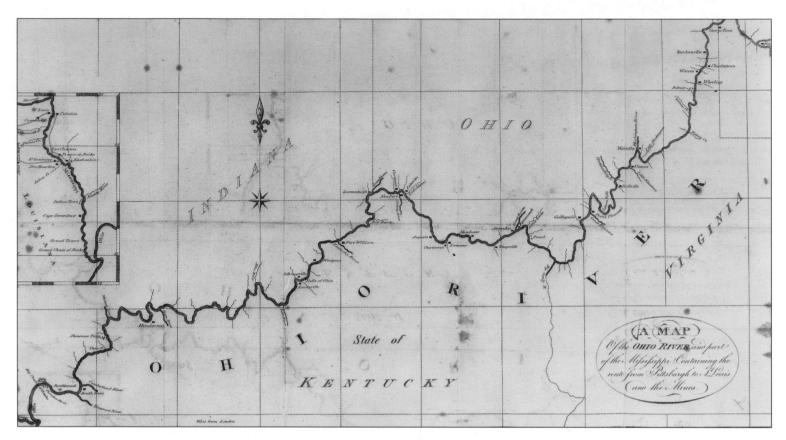

In the 1760s and 1770s the Ohio River was supposed to mark the boundary between settlers' and Native Americans' territories. This map from the 1780s, however, shows settlements and U.S. territory names in the region north of the river. The newly independent nation was swiftly sweeping aside the Native Americans' claims.

Dunmore, the governor of Virginia, called on the frontier settlers to defend themselves, and the settlers took this as a go-ahead for war against the Indians. **Militiamen** crossed the Ohio River to raid Shawnee villages. The Shawnee struck back with an attack on the mili-

tiamen. Kentucky became a "dark and bloody ground," according to Dragging Canoe, a chief of the Cherokee people, who also hunted there. Lord Dunmore's War ended when the Shawnee asked for peace, fearing further destruction of their villages. The Shawnee agreed to stay out of

By the time of the American Revolution (1776–1783), the original Native American population of the East Coast had all but disappeared. From Maine to the Carolinas, Indians had died of diseases brought by the colonists or had been pushed off their land. In the years between 1750 and 1783, colonists inched north and west, even though the British tried to set a limit to settlement at the crest of the Appalachians. After the Revolution, Americans surged westward, gobbling up huge tracts of Native American land in the fertile valleys of the Ohio and Mississippi rivers. The American settler population steadily increased, leaving the Indians of the region with three choices. They could move west into other Indians' territory, they could abandon their traditional way of life and try to exist among the white settlers as farmers or workers—or they could fight.

LAND TAKEN FROM THE NATIVE AMERICANS 1750-1810

Land taken before 1750

Land taken 1750-1783

Land taken 1784-1810

PENOBSCOT

ABNAKI

IROQUOIS

WAMPANOAG

NARRAGANSETT

ERIE

PEQUOT

MOHEGAN

MIAMI

SUSQUEHANNA

LENI-LENAPE

MISSOURI

ILLINOIS

KANSAS

KICKAPOO

Ohio

POWHATAN

OSAGE

SHAWNEE

CHEROKEE

Mississippi

Red

CREEK

Atlantic

Ocean

CHICKASAW

NATCHEZ

SEMINOLE

Gulf of Mexico

0   250 miles

0   500 kms

© Oxford Cartographers

Lake Superior

Lake Michigan

Lake Huron

Lake Ontario

Lake Erie

St. Lawrence

Kentucky, and the whites agreed to stay out of Ohio. Neither side would keep its word.

The Wilderness Road

Now that Kentucky seemed open for settlement, Judge Richard Henderson of North Carolina wasted no time. He was a speculator who claimed to have bought most of Kentucky and part of Tennessee from the Cherokee Indians—even though the British government had not authorized him to do so. But Henderson didn't let a little thing like the law stop him. He hired a frontiersman and hunter named Daniel Boone to **pioneer** a route into Kentucky from the south.

Boone and his thirty axe-wielding comrades hacked their way from Virginia westward through the Cumberland Gap, the only good pass through the Appalachians south of Pennsylvania. The route they created came to be called the Wilderness Road. Later it would be wide and well-traveled, pressed flat by the wagon wheels of thousands of settlers headed west. But for this first group of settlers it was just a rough, narrow trail that ended at a point on the south bank of the Kentucky River. There, in 1775, Boone founded a settlement he called Boonesborough.

Henderson's dream was that his land grant would become a new colony, Transylvania (from the Latin words for "beyond the forest"). If he had succeeded, the United States might

Some Americans saw Daniel Boone (1734-1820), survivor of Indian skirmishes and founder of one of the first Ohio Valley settlements, as a symbol of their heroic progress westward.

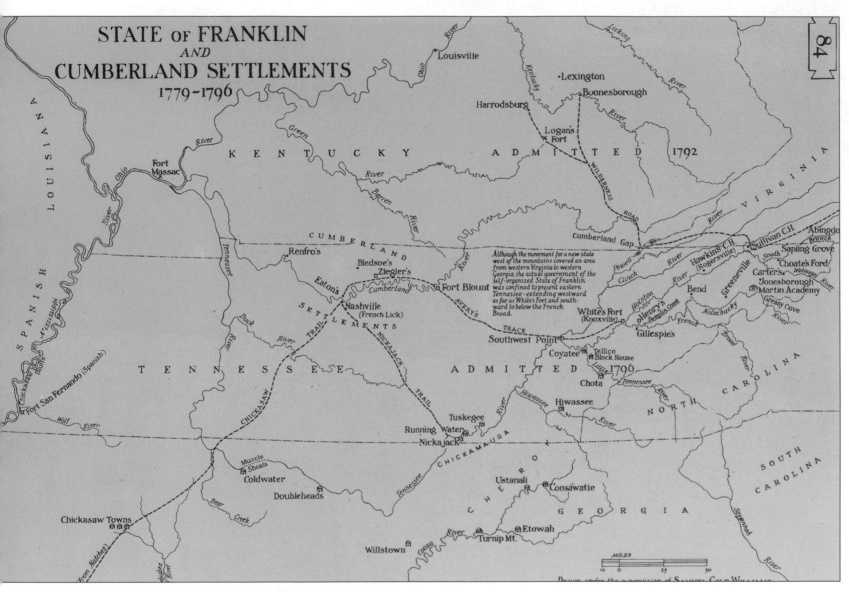

Although the movement for a new state west of the mountains covered an area from western Virginia to western Georgia, the actual government of the self-organized State of Franklin was confined to present eastern Tennessee—extending westward as far as White's Fort and southward to below the French Broad.

A map of western settlements in the late eighteenth century shows the Wilderness Road from the Cumberland Gap to Boonesborough and the settlements along the Cumberland River. In the 1780s, settlers in North Carolina's western territory called their region the "state of Franklin." Congress never recognized this "state," which eventually became Tennessee.

now have a state called Transylvania. The existing colonial governments, however, regarded Henderson's Cherokee treaty as illegal, and Kentucky came under Virginia's rule.

In the meantime, the settlers at Boonesborough had problems of their own: food shortages, Indian attacks, and disagreements among themselves. They had little time or energy to spare for news from the eastern colonies, where rebellion against Great Britain was brewing. But when the Revolutionary War broke out, and the British began urging Native American warriors to attack the frontier settlements, the settlers quickly decided to support the revolutionary cause. And even while the war was raging, farmers and families continued to come west along the Wilderness Road—as many as 20,000 people, drawn by the lure of cheap land and a new beginning.

Chapter Two

THE
NORTHWEST
TERRITORY

On the Road

After the United States won independence from Great Britain, the trickle of settlers crossing the Appalachians swelled into a flood. The westward road was not an easy one, however, and the western territory was far from peaceful. Americans entering the Ohio River Valley met two sets of enemies: the Native Americans, who resented being pushed off their traditional lands by settlers, and the British, who hated the thought of giving up the region to the United States. These two forces sometimes joined together against the Americans in the hard-fought-for land called the Northwest Territory.

U.S. Territory in 1783

When the Revolutionary War ended in 1783, the new United States received everything south of the Great Lakes and east of the Mississippi—excellent news for speculators and settlers. But the British still had

Canada, and they still occupied some forts at key locations on the American frontier, such as Niagara and Detroit. They could—and would—continue to stir up trouble for the United States.

An even bigger problem was the Native Americans, who had no voice in the agreement that the British and the Americans made in Paris to divide up the frontier. The Indians did not recognize the new U.S. claim to the Ohio

After the rough frontier trails had been widened and flattened into primitive roads, settlers could haul their goods in Conestoga wagons, named for the Pennsylvania town where they were manufactured after about 1750. Settled communities became used to the sight of pioneer caravans heading toward the beckoning frontier.

Dragging Canoe, a chief of the Native American Cherokee people, called Kentucky "a dark and bloody ground" because of the violent deeds that had taken place there during the fighting between Indians and settlers. The same phrase describes the whole Northwest Territory, the name that Congress gave to the region north of the Ohio River in 1787. Dotted with rival British and American forts, occupied by a dozen or more Native American peoples who were increasingly desperate to halt the flood of settlers, the Northwest Territory would remain a battle-ground for years. In addition to the two

THE NORTHWEST TERRITORY

	The Northwest Territory
★	British Posts held until 1796
★	U.S. Posts
⚔	Battle Site

major battles between Indians and American settlers in Ohio, there were countless conflicts, raids, and skirmishes. From their bases in Canada, the British maintained forts, agents, and spies in the Northwest Territory long after that region passed into the hands of the United States.

On the Road

Crossing a River

Frontier settlement was not for the weak. It demanded long hours of toil from every family member. But although frontier folk took pride in their sturdy independence, they also tended to form strong communities. Neighbors relied on each other's help in everything from building a barn to birthing a baby.

country. The stage was set for further conflict, especially when the British encouraged the Indians to attack settlers and provided them with weapons.

Desperate to keep the onrushing tide of Amer-

icans out of the Ohio River valley and the Great Lakes region, some Indians turned for help to the British, who had been their enemies just twenty years earlier during the French and Indian War. The British, in turn, wanted to cause as much trouble as possible for the Americans, and Indian wars were an excellent way to do so. British officers supplied guns and ammunition to the Native Americans at the forts that Great Britain maintained in what was officially U.S. territory. By the end of the Revolutionary War in 1783 the British presence was stronger in the Ohio country than it had been before the war. Conflict there would eventually become one of the main causes of the War of 1812 between Great Britain and the United States.

To the west and south, the United States was bordered by Spanish territory. Spain claimed everything between the Mississippi River and the Pacific Ocean. It also controlled the Floridas, a territory that included not just present-day Florida but the Gulf Coast all the way to the mouth of the Mississippi. Spain could cause trouble if Americans pushed west of the Mississippi, and it could also make it difficult for the United States to use the lower Mississippi and the port of New Orleans for trade.

The States Stake Their Claims

After the French and Indian War the British had faced two problems regarding the **trans-Appalachian** frontier: how to deal with the

TIDY TOWNSHIPS

Congress passed a law called the Ordinance of 1785 that outlined the way land in the territory north of the Ohio River would be surveyed and sold. The land would be divided into square townships six miles (10 kilometers) long and six miles (10 kilometers) wide. Each township would contain thirty-six square sections, and each section would contain 640 acres (250 hectares). The federal government would auction off the land by section. Speculators could afford to buy whole sections, but few farmers could do so—which meant that speculators could make a profit by breaking up sections into smaller parcels and selling those parcels to settlers.

Some of the eastern states claimed that their original charters, dating from the time the colonies were founded, had no western borders. These states argued that they extended west all the way to the Mississippi River or even the Pacific Ocean. If the federal government had listened to these arguments, the United States might now consist of half a dozen short but very wide states stacked like the layers of a cake. The greediest states were Virginia and New York. Each claimed an enormous stretch of western land far beyond any reasonable extension of its borders. In the end, though, the states turned their western claims over to the federal government, which eventually turned them into territories and then new states. The caption lists the years in which each eastern state gave up all or part of its claim.

The township-and-section system was a neat, orderly plan for the settling of the northwestern frontier. If you fly low over Ohio or Indiana today you can see how well the plan worked. Much of the land is still divided into square patterns by roads that follow the old township and section boundaries.

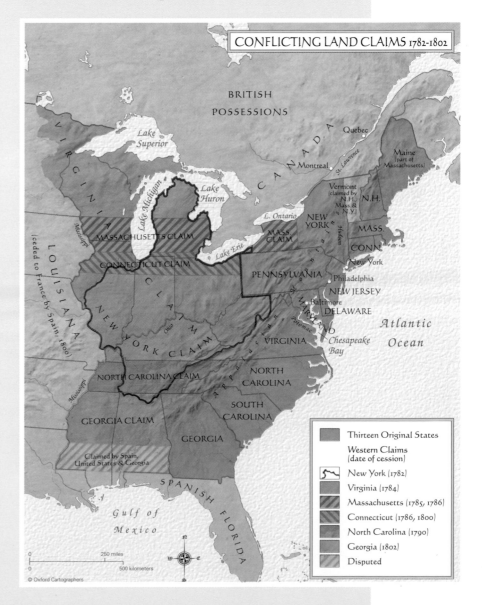

CONFLICTING LAND CLAIMS 1782-1802

Thirteen Original States

Western Claims (date of cession)

New York (1782)

Virginia (1784)

Massachusetts (1785, 1786)

Connecticut (1786, 1800)

North Carolina (1790)

Georgia (1802)

Disputed

© Oxford Cartographers

Indians and how to organize settlement. Unable to solve those problems, they had tried to hold them off with the Proclamation of 1763. Now the new U.S. government faced the same problems—and they could not be put off any longer. By 1783 nearly 100,000 Americans lived on the western frontier. Many of them were "squatters," who settled wherever they wanted without bothering about land ownership. Often disorderly, the region was in danger of becoming an independent country, or perhaps even a Spanish territory. Congress had to act.

But who owned the frontier? Of the original thirteen states, seven claimed that their territory stretched into the new western lands. Some claims clashed or overlapped—New York, for example, claimed a vast tract, parts of which were also claimed by Connecticut, Massachusetts, and Virginia. The six states that *didn't* have claims felt that the whole trans-Appalachian region should belong to the federal government. Realizing that controlling and governing the western territories would be a difficult and expensive task, the states with land claims reluctantly agreed.

The Northwest Ordinance

In 1787 the U.S. Congress passed a law called the Northwest Ordinance that organized the region north of the Ohio River and east of the Mississippi into an administrative unit called the Northwest Territory. The ordinance also declared that the Northwest Territory could be divided into three to five smaller territories that would someday become states. Eventually, the Northwest Territory would become five states: Ohio, Indiana, Illinois, Michigan, and Wisconsin.

As for government, at first Congress would name a governor, a secretary, and three judges to make laws for each territory. Once a territory had 5,000 inhabitants, it could elect a legislature. And once it had 60,000 people, it could ask Congress to make the territory a state. The Northwest Ordinance did more than just establish the Northwest Territory. It set the pattern for territorial organization and government that settlers would follow throughout the 1800s as the United States moved west all the way to the Pacific Ocean.

War on the Frontier

There were just two problems with the Ordinance of 1785 and the Northwest Ordinance. One problem was the great number of squatters who illegally occupied land, despite the government's efforts to force them back with troops. The other problem was getting ownership of the land in Ohio and Indiana from the Native Americans.

The federal government followed a program of "buying" land from Indian chiefs through agreements called treaties. The problem with such deals was that most of the chiefs who signed the treaties did not actually own the land they

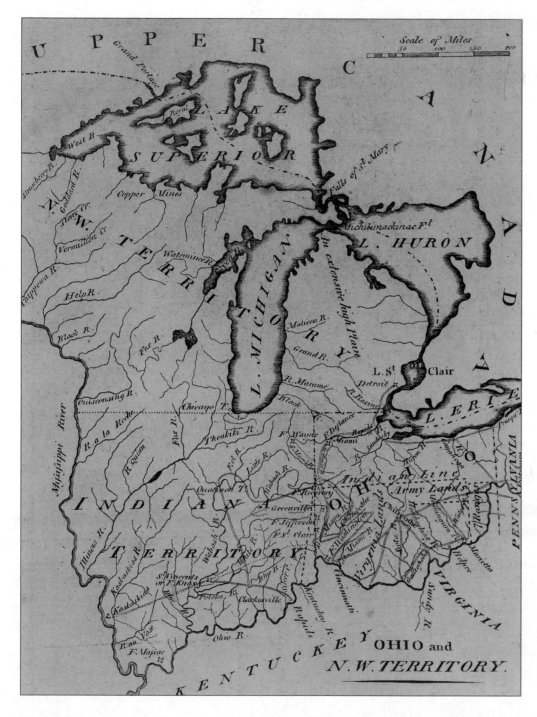

Ohio was the first state created from the Northwest Territory. This early map shows roads crisscrossing Ohio and snaking west into the Indiana Territory, which would eventually become the states of Indiana and Illinois. Wisconsin, in the far northwestern part of the territory, has no settlements yet, although the map shows the location of copper mines along the shore of Lake Superior.

General Arthur St. Clair started his military career as a British officer, then switched sides in the middle of the American Revolution. The U.S. government rewarded him by making him governor of the Northwest Territory, but he failed dismally to control the Native Americans there. When he met them in battle he lost more than half his 1,400-man army. The Indians lost twenty-one warriors.

were "selling." Other Indians refused to honor the treaties. To make matters worse, even when Indians accepted a treaty line separating their land from the white settlers' land, the settlers could not be counted on to remain on their side of the line. With every push onto Indian land came more raids by Indians on settlements and more revenge attacks on Indian villages by white militia, continuing the vicious cycle.

Determined to end the fighting, President George Washington sent an army into the Northwest under General Arthur St. Clair in 1791. The Indians soundly defeated St. Clair's army. The next general Washington sent, Anthony Wayne, was a much better leader. He defeated the Indians at the Battle of Fallen Timbers in 1794 and forced them to sign the Treaty of Greenville the next year. Under this treaty, the Indians gave up most of Ohio and part of Indiana. The wiser among them realized that eventually they would be forced to yield the rest of the Northwest Territory as well.

General Anthony Wayne proved a far better frontier fighter than St. Clair. Mounted on his white horse, Wayne led his army to victory over Native American forces at the Battle of Fallen Timbers, a place in northwestern Ohio where a storm had toppled many trees.

Chapter Three

TO THE
MISSISSIPPI
AND BEYOND

An eagle flying from the Appalachians to the Mississippi River in the 1790s would have soared over a vast, wild forest, broken only by a few trails, with threads of smoke rising here and there from a few scattered Indian villages and settler homesteads. In 1840, a bird flying over the same region would have looked down on a settled part of the United States, a patchwork quilt of farmland, dotted with many towns, crisscrossed by wagon roads and canals. The frontier spirit wasn't dead, however; it had just moved on. By the time America's first frontier was settled, its people were already looking west beyond the Mississippi River to the next frontier.

Americans in Spanish Territory

While General Wayne was dealing with the Native Americans in the Northwest Territory, another crisis was brewing on the border between Spanish and American territory along the Mississippi. Spain controlled the great

"I am overjoyed that we all passed safely through many hazards," one pioneer woman wrote in her journal after a hair-raising flatboat trip on the Ohio and Mississippi rivers. Other travelers were less lucky. Their accounts tell of overturned boats, drowned livestock, and other disasters.

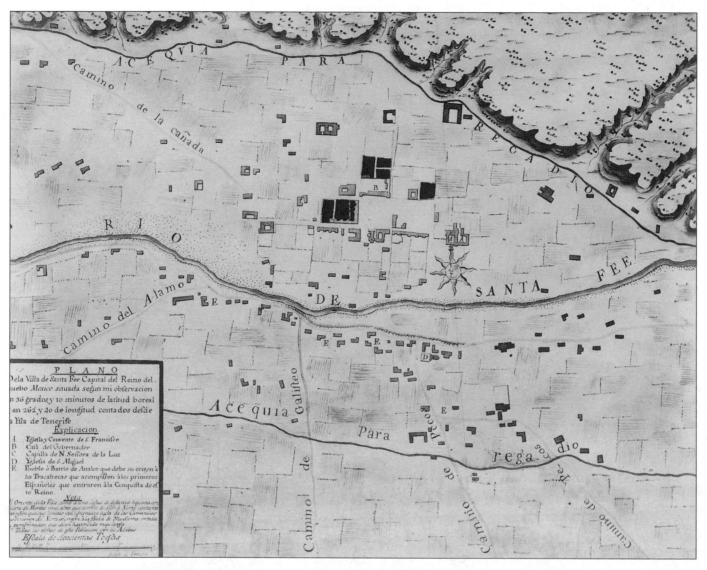

This old Spanish map depicts the farms and buildings of early Santa Fe, New Mexico, a settlement older than any British colony. Even before the Americans had finished struggling with Great Britain for control of eastern North America, they knew that Spain claimed the western part of the continent. One way or another, they would have to come to terms with the Spanish.

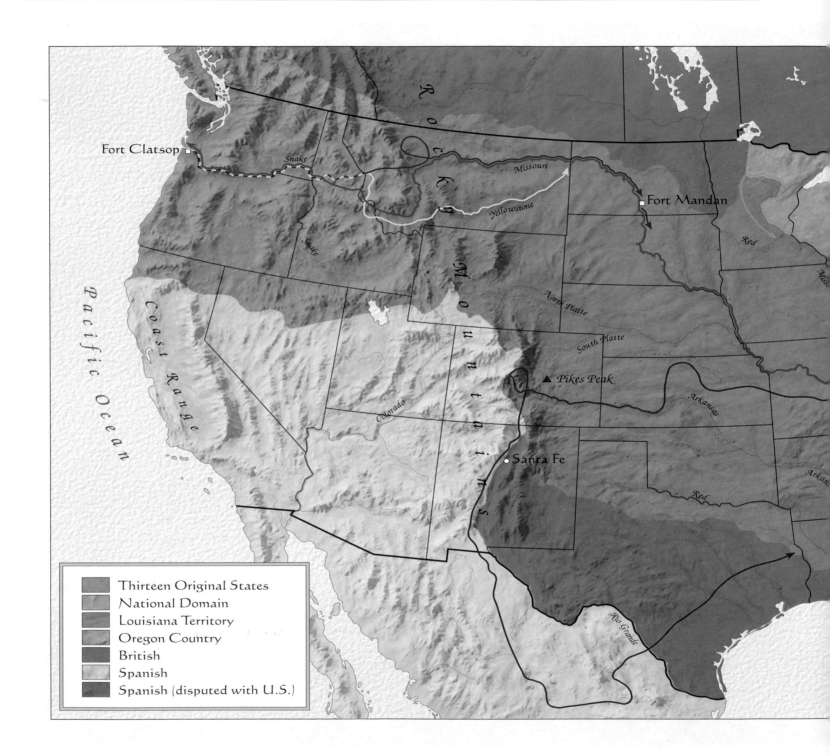

Fort Clatsop

Fort Mandan

Rocky

Snake

Missouri

Yellowstone

Mountains

Snake

North Platte

South Platte

Pacific Ocean

Coast Range

▲ Pikes Peak

Arkansas

Colorado

○ Santa Fe

Red

Arkansas

Red

Rio Grande

Thirteen Original States
National Domain
Louisiana Territory
Oregon Country
British
Spanish
Spanish (disputed with U.S.)

The Louisiana Purchase did more than add the land between the Mississippi River and the Rocky Mountains to the United States. It also opened this vast region to American explorers. Two of the most important exploring expeditions, however, ventured well beyond U.S. borders. In the north, the Lewis and Clark expedition journeyed through the newly acquired Louisiana territory and continued to the Pacific Ocean through the region that came to be called the Oregon Country. The British were also exploring the Oregon Country from the north, and the United States and Great Britain would share that corner of North America for years to come. Zebulon Pike also explored the northern edge of the Louisiana territory, but his most famous exploring mission took him much farther south, into Spanish territory. The Spanish captured Pike and his men, accusing them of being spies, but Pike claimed that they had simply gotten lost. When the Spanish released him, he returned to the United States with information on the geography, resources, and military posts of the Spanish territory he had crossed.

river, which was vital to settlers who wanted to get their products to foreign markets, but Spain often closed the river to American traffic. By the 1790s, a number of Americans had moved into the lands along the lower Mississippi and even into the Spanish-owned Gulf Coast. They realized that without the free use of the Ohio-Mississippi waterway system, the economy of the trans-Appalachian region could not develop.

Some Americans, upset that their government was not doing more to loosen Spain's hold on the Mississippi, formed their own plans. In 1794, a number of angry Americans, led by a revolutionary from France, joined a plot to form a private army to capture Florida and Louisiana from Spain. One of the plotters was George Rogers Clark, a hero of the Revolutionary War on the frontier. President Washington learned of the plot in time to end it by passing a law that banned private armies. The following year, the U.S. signed a treaty with Spain that guaranteed Americans the right to use the Mississippi River. It also opened the land on the east side of the lower Mississippi to American settlement.

Settlers quickly poured into the region. Some traveled overland in large, creaking, canvas-topped wagons, hauling their household goods over a southern arm of the Wilderness Road called the Natchez Trace. Others floated down the Ohio River and then the broad, muddy Mississippi on flatboats, bringing all their live-stock and household goods with them. Soon settlements were taking root all along the eastern bank of the Mississippi. To the west, beyond the river, lay Spanish territory—but not for long.

An Unbeatable Deal

Spain needed money and was willing to sell the Louisiana Territory to France, which had established the first settlements along the lower Mississippi in the 1600s. In 1800, France acquired a huge region north of Texas, between the Mississippi River and the Rocky Mountains. Rumors of this deal alarmed the Americans, who feared that France would be much less generous with **navigation** rights on the Mississippi than Spain had been.

President Thomas Jefferson decided to try to buy New Orleans and the Floridas from France. To his amazement, Napoleon Bonaparte, the ruler of France, offered him a much bigger piece of land—the entire Louisiana Territory. In what ranks as one of the smartest real-estate buys of all time, Jefferson paid France $15 million in what has come to be known as the Louisiana Purchase. This deal doubled the size of the United States overnight! No longer was the Mississippi River the final frontier of the American settler.

The Corps of Discovery

Even before the Louisiana Purchase, Jefferson had been planning to send explorers into the

Meriwether Lewis (1776–1809) was Thomas Jefferson's choice to lead the first American expedition to cross the continent. Lewis decided to share the leadership with another army officer, William Clark. Together the two led one of the best-managed and most successful exploring expeditions in history.

British to develop exploration and trade routes in the Rocky Mountains and the Pacific Northwest, and Jefferson was determined not to let Great Britain have the northwestern corner of the continent to itself.

Once the Louisiana Purchase was made, Jefferson ordered Army officers Meriwether Lewis and William Clark to lead an expedition called the Corps of Discovery across the western lands to the Pacific Ocean and back—a journey no American had yet made. The Corps had several missions. One was to gather scientific and geographic information. Another was to establish friendly relations with the Native American tribes along the way. And a third mission was to show both Britain and Spain that the United States had a claim to the Pacific Northwest.

The Corps of Discovery consisted of about forty-five men, led by the two officers. The expedition left St. Louis on the Mississippi River in the spring of 1804. Its route ran up the Missouri River into western Montana, across the Rocky Mountains of Montana and Idaho, and down the Clearwater, Snake, and Columbia rivers to the Pacific Ocean. After spending a damp, fogbound winter in a fort they built on the Pacific shore, the travelers returned to St. Louis, where they arrived to a great pealing of church bells in the fall of 1806.

The Lewis and Clark expedition completed all of its missions. The explorers had mapped a route to the Pacific coast, gathered hundreds

lands beyond the Mississippi. Jefferson, who was greatly interested in geography and science, was very curious about the little-known western part of North America. His interest rose when he read the *Voyages* of Alexander Mackenzie, a Scottish explorer who had crossed Canada from Montreal to the Pacific Ocean. Mackenzie was urging the

Upon reaching the Pacific coast, the Lewis and Clark expedition built a fort in which to spend the winter. They named it Fort Clatsop after a local Indian tribe. Although the exact location of their fort is unknown, a replica stands today near Astoria, Oregon.

of samples of rocks, plants, and animals, and written volumes of notes about the weather, resources, and Indians of the west. They had also staked an American claim to the fertile, attractive region known as the Oregon Country along the Columbia River.

Pike and His Peak

Even before the Corps returned to St. Louis, another young Army officer was also probing the Far West. His name was Zebulon Pike, and he was not just an explorer—he was also a spy.

In 1805, at the age of twenty-six, Pike headed north up the Mississippi River and established a U.S. claim to the territory that became

SACAJAWEA

Lewis and Clark hired a number of trappers and **voyageurs** to guide them west. One of them, Louis Charbonneau, asked if his Native American wife, Sacajawea, could accompany the expedition. Lewis and Clark reluctantly agreed. Later, however, Clark would admit that Sacajawea was more dependable and useful to the expedition than her husband.

Much mythology has grown up around the figure of Sacajawea. She was not the expedition's guide, as she has sometimes been described. She did, however, perform valuable service as an **interpreter** when the explorers met a group of Shoshone Indians, including Sacajawea's own brother. Little is known of Sacajawea's life after the expedition. Even the date and place of her death are uncertain. But the recollections of her by William Clark and other expedition members paint an unforgettable picture of a brave, resourceful, and capable woman explorer.

Sacajawea, who accompanied the Lewis and Clark expedition, was a woman of the Shoshone people, who lived in the northern Rocky Mountains. She was the first woman known to have crossed the western United States, and she did so while caring for a baby.

Zebulon Pike was bold and resourceful—
good qualities for an explorer or a spy.
He made notes on everything he saw
in Spanish territory and then smuggled
the notes past his captors by stuffing
them into the barrels of his men's rifles.

Minnesota. The following year, an Army general named James Wilkenson—who later turned out to have taken bribes from the Spanish—sent Pike on a mission into the Southwest, where the United States and Spain were quarreling about territorial borders. Some historians believe that Wilkenson wanted the two countries to go to war so that, in the confusion, he and his followers could form a private army and seize Louisiana. Pike did not know the details of this plan. He simply followed Wilkenson's orders.

In following those orders, Pike ventured into a region that was claimed by both the United States and Spain. The territory was south of the Red River and north of the Rio Grande. Here, he knowingly and illegally entered Spanish territory. The Spanish captured him but treated him well and eventually let him go. If Wilkenson had been hoping for war, he was disappointed. Upon his return to the United States, Pike gave a detailed and lively account of the Spanish settlement of Santa Fe in New Mexico, inspiring several hardy frontier traders to set out on the hazardous overland route from St. Louis to Santa Fe. He also reported on a giant Rocky Mountain peak that he and his men had spotted. Today that Colorado mountain is called Pikes Peak in his honor.

Settlement and Statehood

In 1818, Samuel Crabtree, an English settler in the Ohio Valley, wrote to his brother that "this is the country for a man to enjoy himself…Ohio, Indiana, and the Missouri Territory…I believe I saw more peaches and apples rotting on the ground than would sink the British fleet." People marveled at the richness and fertility of the land on the frontier, and they scrambled to buy it up. By 1820, two million people, one-fifth of the total population of the United States, lived west of the Appalachians.

By 1803, Kentucky, Tennessee, and Ohio had become states. Other territories would follow. The trans-Appalachian region, once a dark and dangerous frontier, was becoming quite

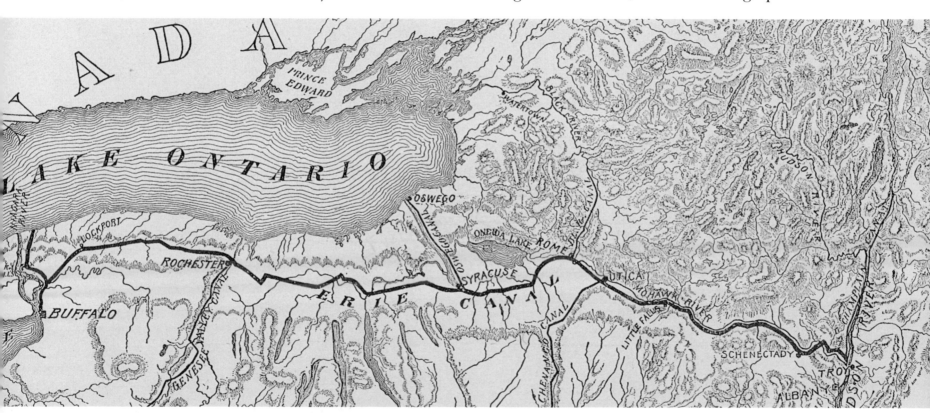

The Erie Canal was one of the first big public engineering projects in the United States.
In time, many other canals branched off it to form a transportation network that
would play a vital role in the industrial development of the northeastern states.

civilized. Roads built by private companies connected many frontier regions with the Atlantic coast. These roads were known as turnpikes or toll roads, and travelers had to pay to use them. But the federal government built the National Road, the nation's first highway, to connect Baltimore with Ohio, then extended the road through Indiana and into Illinois.

The regions on either side of the Appalachians were also linked by a water route, thanks to the Erie Canal, which opened in 1825. It connected the Atlantic Ocean and the Hudson River to the Great Lakes. Eventually, other canals linked the Great Lakes to the Mississippi, creating a system of waterways for freight and passengers that spanned the eastern United States.

By the time the National Road and the Erie Canal were completed, the land between the Appalachians and the Mississippi River was largely settled. But some restless souls, following in the footsteps of Lewis and Clark and of Pike, were already moving west, carrying the frontier with them.

Lockport, in western New York near Niagara Falls, grew up around one of the Erie Canal's locks, a chamber in which boats were raised or lowered to move between bodies of water at different levels. The people who lived and worked in Lockport helped maintain a link between the markets of the East Coast and a frontier that was moving ever farther west.

London mapmaker John Cary published this map of North America in 1811. Maps had become less ornamental than those of the 17th and 18th century. Gone are the sea serpents, animals, and Native American villages with which early mapmakers decorated the continent. But Cary possessed more accurate and complete information about North America than the earlier mapmakers had had. His map is correct in many details. It shows that settlement was still concentrated along the coasts and in the eastern part of the United States. This region between the Mississippi River and the Pacific Ocean, which Lewis and Clark had crossed a few years before Carey created this map, remains largely unknown. To the south, Mexico's interior is fully settled and mapped after three centuries of colonization by the Spanish. To the north, fur-trading posts and small settlements string into the interior of Canada. Farther north still, the map trails off into uncertain guesswork about the unexplored lands on the shore of the "Icy Sea."

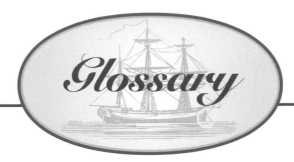

Glossary

frontier: The boundary between wilderness and settled territory.

game: Wild animals and birds that can be hunted for food.

interpreter: Someone who speaks two languages and assists communication between people who speak only one or the other of the languages.

migration: The movement of groups or individuals from one region or homeland to another.

militiamen: Citizens authorized to arm themselves and act as soldiers in times of emergency.

navigation: Shipping.

pioneer: Someone who is among the first to do something or go somewhere; to launch a trend or be a pioneer.

speculator: Someone who buys large quantities of land, expecting to make a profit by selling smaller pieces of it at higher prices to those who will actually live on and work the land.

trans-Appalachian: Beyond, or west of, the Appalachian mountains.

voyageur: A French-Canadian trader or trapper who traveled long distances along wilderness rivers in a canoe or boat; a "voyager."

Map List

ABOUT THE HISTORICAL MAPS

The historical maps used in this book are primary source documents found in The Library of Congress Map Division. You will find these maps on pages 12, 13, 16, 25, 31, and 42–43.

Chronology

1763   Great Britain tries to prevent colonists from settling west of the Appalachian Mountains.

1774   Lord Dunmore's War against the Shawnee opens Kentucky to white settlers.

1787   U.S. Congress creates the Northwest Territory.

1792   Kentucky becomes a state.

1795   U.S. government acquires former Native American lands in the Northwest Territory under the Treaty of Greenville.

1796   Tennessee becomes a state.

1803   Ohio becomes a state. United States buys the Louisiana Purchase from France.

1804–1806   Lewis and Clark lead the first American overland expedition to the Pacific coast.

1812   Great Britain and the United States go to war, with major fighting in the Northwest Territory and on the Gulf Coast.

Further Reading

Cavan, Seamus. *Daniel Boone and the Opening of the Ohio Country.* New York: Chelsea House, 1991.

Cavan, Seamus. *Lewis and Clark and the Route to the Pacific.* New York: Chelsea House, 1991.

Derleth, August. *Vincennes: Portal to the West.* Englewood Cliffs, NJ: Prentice-Hall, 1968.

Hargrove, Jim. *Daniel Boone: Pioneer Trailblazer.* Chicago: Childrens Press, 1985.

Lawlor, Laurie. *Daniel Boone.* Niles, IL: Whitman, 1988.

Marrin, Albert. *1812: The War Nobody Won.* New York: Atheneum, 1985.
Morris, Richard B. *The War of 1812.* Minneapolis: Lerner Publications: 1985.

Rohrbough, Malcolm J. *The Trans-Appalachian Frontier.* New York: Oxford University Press, 1978.

Wexler, Sanford. *Westward Expansion.* New York: Facts On File, 1991.

WEBSITES

www.heidelberg.edu/FallenTimbers (Battle of Fallen Timbers)

www.history.rochester.edu/canal (History of the Erie Canal)

www.loc.gov/rr/geogmap/guide (The Library of Congress Geography and Maps: An Illustrated Guide)

www.louisville.edu/library/ekstrom/govpubs/states/kentucky/kyhistory/boone.html (Daniel Boone)

www.nps.gov/lecl (Lewis and Clark National Historical Trail)

ABOUT THE AUTHOR

Rebecca Stefoff is the author of many nonfiction books for young readers, including a number of volumes on American exploration, settlement, and history. Although she now lives in Portland, Oregon, she grew up in Fort Wayne, Indiana, in the heart of the Old Northwest Territory, surrounded by memorials to the era of frontier settlement.

Index

Entries are filed letter-by-letter. Page numbers for illustrations and maps are in boldface.